THE GOD DILEMMA

DESIGN OR CHANCE

N. K. ANING

ISBN 979-888606244-1

I dedicte this book to you, the readers. May you get some knowledegeable thing to know about your life. Also, I dedicate this book to all my family members for their positive support and helping me in completion of this very book. Really thankful to you all.

Contents

Foreword *vii*

Preface *ix*

1. Have An Eagle's Attitude 1
2. Mentality 3
3. The Most Memorable Moment In My Life 5
4. Be Ready To Fight With Challenges 7
5. Great Things Take Time 8
6. Have Patience 10
7. Try To Enjoy Every Second Of Your Life 11
8. Be A Struggler 13
9. Utilize Your Life 15
10. Life -to- Death, Don't Waste Your “to” 16
11. What And Where Beauty Is? 18
12. Positivity 19
13. Serve Humanity 21
14. Find Beauty Everywhere 23
15. Get Good At Asking 25

Author's Request 27

Foreword

This book relates to different lessons , life taught me till date. Its the summation of all my experience gained from life as well as time. These things played a very crucial role in determining me life goals and setting it. may the readers also get motivated from this and get some benifits in their life, the only thing I pray......

Preface

I Amrit Nanda, a budding writer is persuing my graduation at DSBM, BBSR . I love to write poems and life lessons. The thing I write is totally related to my own life. I started writing the point of time I passed my class 10th. I am much passionate to write. I want to be the author of one of the best-sellers one day.

CHAPTER ONE

HAVE AN EAGLE'S ATTITUDE

Never be a parrot in your life. A parrot can talk but cannot fly high. An eagle cannot talk but, can fly high. Let me convey you all the qualities and mentalities of an eagle, equally to be compared with the human beings. I feel you would get an energetic motivation from my few lines.

1. Eagles fly alone at high altitudes .the eagle doesn't fly with sparrows or with many of the small birds. They only fly with the eagles. This clearly signifies that they stay away from narrow minded elements. It is rightly said that the more time you spend with the kind of people, the more the characteristics of them are present inside you.
2. The eagles have a brilliant vision. They have the ability to focus on their prey even flying five kilometers away. No matter what the obstacle may be but, the eagle won't remove his focus from the prey until he grabs it. Likely, you should have a vision focused on your life. No matter what the obstacles may be. You should have guts to face them.

3. The eagles are fearless. An eagle will never surrender to the size or strength of its prey. It means that no matter what the problems may be, you should have a positive attitude towards it. People aiming to get success, never fear of any obstacles.
4. An Eagle never feeds upon the dead matter. It only eats the meat of the prey, it kills itself. It means that never depend on your past success. Keep looking for new challenges to be faced by you.
5. Eagles prepare for training. They put thorns and dry bushes in their nests so that when their young ones could not able to anymore bear the pain, they will start flying. It means, leave your comfort zone. You will never grow successful using the bed of roses. Comfort kills your future.
6. Eagles create life. When the eagles grow old their feather becomes weak ad they were not able to fly fast and high. In this condition they pluck all their old feathers and break their beaks by rubbing with the rocks .they wait for some time to regain all new feathers and a new sharp Beak. At last, it takes a big flight touching the sky with a happiness of no limits. They celebrate their happiness with a grand scream. All totally, it means that sometimes we need to shed off our old habits to get something new and fantastic.

At last, I would conclude my this piece of writing by conveying you all that having a badass attitude like an eagle helps us to be successful in our life to a great extent. Look eagle in yourselves.............

CHAPTER TWO

MENTALITY

Thinking of something good to happen in life thinking of something bad to happen in life, positive thoughts, dealing with problems in a positive manner, disobeying or disrespecting someone or to be annoyed on someone are something which we call as mentality.

Literally, mentality is omnipresent, its in every creature, in every living being but its best example will be human beings. The mentality of a person well defines his knowledge, relation and comparability skills related to the developments in the recent times. As electronic devices requires updates to be in the latest version , human minds too need to be updated with the latest trends of this developing world.

Let us take an example of a person who is an introvert. People name them as introverts but, its not a disease or an deficiency but a state of mind which people fail to understand. On the other hand an extrovert is open minded and socialistic. What is it? It is the mentality of the specific person. People say that " attitude is the biggest factor in a person's life". But, I will not agree upon it, because attitude is a secondary factor. But, mentality is an internal factor which makes a lots of differences upon the mind of a person.

You might be experiencing a fact that though you have scored ninety plus marks , yet your parents are not satisfies with it. But, a teacher always knows how much a student is capable of. Because it is always said that ''only the wearer knows where the shoe pinches''. Though the teacher teaches the students, he knows the pain and pressure on students.

Similarly, you might have seen that old people do not like girls to wear jeans or to do a job. After seeing a girl wearing jeans or fancy dresses or going out for doing job, they start gossiping about your families that their parents are uneducated, they do not know manners and all that sort of things and which really hurts. This is what mentality is.

Sometimes you may have seen that old people create superstitious situation in our minds that we were bound to believe in it. Though, we know that these are all nonsense but, what to do when mind itself starts pinching that ''are these superstitions true''? and it creates confusion. They make us think, they make us feel too. Even we do not have any freedom to think in a way we want to.

Atlast, I would like to wind up my writing with a piece of note that, the keys of our mind should be all ours and the mentality should be changed so that a equality should be felt.

The very topic my own felt situations, the situations I went through. Although, the topic seems to be very minimal but, when penned in words can make a vast change upon.....

CHAPTER THREE

THE MOST MEMORABLE MOMENT IN MY LIFE

Our life is fully filled with different types of experiences. From the beginning of the life till end. In this time period we experience lots of situations. Some may be excellent, and some may be bad. But, it totally depends on the almighty and time. The time which passes on excellently, bounds us with its feeling of happiness. But on the other hand, the time which passes really disgusting, creates an ill effect on our mind and makes us distressed.

For me the memorable day in my life till date is the day on which I got my first book published with copyright. That day my happiness was of no bound. I felt a spirit of being an author which I haven't even seen in my dreams. The labor I did really paid me a lot that day. The news of my book being published spread in my locality like anything. I was much happy that day.

Literally my father had discouraged me that " your book will not be much effective. He told that people may not even purchase your book". But, I didn't got demotivated. I carried on and at last published my book with a grand success. my book was named as ''LIVES KNOW-HOW By-AMRIT NANDA''.

The very particular day I got to know that without motivation nothing is possible in this world. Only due to confidence and self-motivation, I was able to publish my first book. Motivation plays a very crucial role in everybody's life. Not everybody can motivate but, he can try to get some motivation. you might be thinking that how everyone needs motivation? let me tell you an example that when you visit a gym you might have seen that the gymnasts use music and mirrors for motivation so that the can lift heavy weights. But, I would challenge you that without motivation you cannot lift heavy weights. If also, but not for a longer time. You will get disgusted and not feel free. So, the same case is applied everywhere. Like in your exams, you sports and many other things, motivation is needed everywhere.

On the same day I promised to be the author of one of the bestsellers one day.

At last, I would end my this piece of writing by reminding you all to be positively motivated even in the toughest situations of life. Only then you can win.

SO, BE MOTIVATED AND LIVE YOUR LIFE PEACEFULLY...

CHAPTER FOUR

BE READY TO FIGHT WITH CHALLENGES

If you want to be the best, it goes without saying. The greatest and the hard in the race, they train hard, they put themselves into more pain, they learn more, more failures, more no's, more rejections. If you are ready, be hard. If they do 12, you do 13. If they do 13, you do 14, 15, and 16 and go on with it.

There are many geniuses in this world. But, their genuineness would not have been expressed if they haven't done any labor or beared any pain to be genius. They have created magic with their efforts only.

When life says no, you say yes, yes and yes to get something new every time. If life stops you, kick off your emotions and move along the long race of your life. Fight with yourself, fight with challenges, fight with your emotions and go grab your dreams to make it true.

If you work more, you get more; you feel more, more, more, and more.

More than the most.

CHAPTER FIVE

GREAT THINGS TAKE TIME

1. If you need, you can.
2. Never give up. Great things take time. Be patient.
3. Difficult roads often lead o beautiful destinations.
4. The pain you feel today will be the strength you feel tomorrow.
5. I exist as I am, that is enough.
6. The best way to gain self-confidence is to do what you are afraid to do.
7. 10 years from now, you'll be more disappointed by the things you didn't do.
8. The secret of success is determined by your daily agenda.
9. Hard work is what successful people do.
10. Discipline is not a pain, it is training, and it is your best friend. And it will take care of you like nothing else.
11. People, who are crazy enough to think that they can change the world, are the ones who do it.
12. Success is going from failure to failure. Without losing you can't gain anything.

So, stay calm, work hard and let your success make noise..............................

CHAPTER SIX

HAVE PATIENCE

We live in a time where instant gratification is the fuel of our brain. We are so much busy in getting instant results that we have forgotten to be patient. If you open your facebook, you look for the likes and if you open your Instagram, you look for how many new followers you have gained. With this Smartphone, we are almost in a habit to get instant results. It feels like the similar process of chemical reaction occurs in one's body when he tends to smoke, drink or gamble. We have forgotten our patient. We have also forgotten that things in life don't happen overnight. The most important thing in life requires time to happen. Friendship, love, skills, building relationships, takes time.......

So, learn to be patient and don't run before instant results. Things in a life, you cannot reach in a day, it takes some time. It is not possible to happen in a flick of eyelashes. But, it takes some time. Learn to be patient. Otherwise, you would be always empty within yourself for your whole life and will be never satisfied with your life.

At last, as you all have got an idea that 'good things take time', and the best thing in life requires to you is to be 'patient'.

CHAPTER SEVEN

TRY TO ENJOY EVERY SECOND OF YOUR LIFE

Let us have a calculation of time. As we all know, we all sleep eight hours a day. When we were young, we slept for ten – twelve hours a day. When we will be young we will sleep about eight hours a day. But, if an average is taken we sleep about eight hours a day. That means we sleep one-third of twenty four hours in sleeping. If a person expects to live sixty years, he will sleep one-third of his life i.e. twenty years, putting all other things apart.

Do you know a thing that actual time left with us is very less? The survey of Harvard University about asking people that "what according to you is the biggest joy upon this earth"? You would be very much surprised by the feedback of the people. About sixty seven per-cent people said "spending valuable time with near and dear ones is the best joy for them in this earth".

We all have to manage our time. We are the real time managers of our life. We know how to spend our time well. But, we are not utilizing this concept into our life. We have to maintain the balance of life .Make time management a habit in you. Be positive, respect time and live your life fully ....

CHAPTER EIGHT

BE A STRUGGLER

I want you to think about, what you feel when you get dressed up or you put on a new suit and go to an event? And I want you to think about how you feel, how successful you feel even if you're not? What if you woke up every single day with the same confidence? And what if you woke up every single day feeling like the worst chap in this society? And you walk around with that, everywhere you went. How different your life would be? How different your relations would be? How different your career would be? You may not be able to imagine that. But, that's the point of fact.

But how do we translate all these things in our day to day life? Because even people, who wear suits, know that if you wear suit every day, it loses its lusture. It's not the dress; it's not the suit, which makes you feel great. But, it's your pride and attitude which makes it something different from others. And this is how successful people cultivate their feelings over the course of their everyday life.

You have to understand that this shows how you're living up to the standards that you hold for your heart, in your mentality .You should accept the struggle of life. Struggle is a privilege; it's a pride of yourself. You should never think about quitting in your life. Negativity should be killed by your mind.

At last, I would like to say that, `` you are not just enduring your struggle, but chasing your dreams to happen true". So, Accept struggle and get success.

CHAPTER NINE

UTILIZE YOUR LIFE

Life, how beautiful it is? What makes life so unique and so beautiful? It is because, whatever you have that you may be facing or dealing with, make your life good. Life is always good. Every day is a day full of new opportunities that others may not even have.

Life has a deeper meaning. Many people's take life liberally. Now, on this journey of life, you are going to face lots of complications, you are going to fall into situations you have gone through never before. And if you think life as a ruin then, shame on you to say these sorts of things. You have right on your life. Nobody else has any right on your life.

Your life is yours. And you have the right to live your life fully and a way you want to live. You must be disciplined. You should not give up making your life fantastically utilized.

CHAPTER TEN

LIFE -TO- DEATH, DON'T WASTE YOUR "TO"

I want you all to think about when you go to a graveyard for a minute, on the tomb you will find the person's name, the date of birth, a dash and when the person died. Don't you think it to be interesting? The whole life from your birth till death comes to a dash. So, here I wanna ask you that, what do you did during this 'to'?

It is because when you will remember about your dash when you will be 75- 80 years old; there will be nothing left with you other than a handful of regrets. The dash is the time between your birth and death. Life is passing out of our hands in a very fact pace. Nobody knows how many days will we live. Every second we use cannot be backed in our lives.

We have 24 hours in a day and 7 days in a week. Some people simply waste time and some try to live every second of their lifetime is too valuable to be waste. And if you don't believe that, then wait till you 60's or 70's and then you will know about what time is. Life is not totally dependent on money, it's not totally dependent on having a nice bungalow. No, not at all. People in your life are more important than these fellow things. Name, fame and prestige are all secondary components of our life. But, our near and dear ones really make much value for our life.

God had made us to spend most of our time here, getting ready for there. And there when we stand in front of god and give the account of your life, your head should not bend down with regret.

God has given us a single life and a single dash. So, fill your 'to' beautifully and live your life fully.

CHAPTER ELEVEN

WHAT AND WHERE BEAUTY IS?

WHAT BEAUTY IS?
It's the attitude,
which makes us proud.
It's the highlight of your delight.
It's the mirror,
Which reflects as your clone.
It's an expression,
Which helps in exchange of impression.
And also a confidence,
Helping you to kill your incompetence.
BUT,
WHERE BEAUTY IS?
Beauty is there, where health is.
Beauty is there, where you are.
Beauty is there, where you were
And where you tend to be in future.
Beauty is present everywhere, its omnipresent
Because, beauty is there where beauty is.......

CHAPTER TWELVE

POSITIVITY

The word positivity is well-defined by its tone of speaking. It creates a fresh feeling of being positive in our life. Taking as a story of Saint Gaur Gopal Das, I would be very happy to explain you all about the very term "positivity".

One day in a hot summer afternoon, Gaur Gopal Das made a mind to prepare some lemonade and have it. During making the lemonade, one of his friends called him and he was left busy talking with him. Along it talking with his friend, he was making the lemonade. Due to lack of attention, he added four lemons in a glass of water. When the call ended and he went to take a sip of lemonade, he found that the lemonade was so sour that if put in the mouth of a dead body can make it alive again. Its sourness had no words to be defined.

Here comes the point of life, where he added three more glasses of water to the lemonade to make it neutral. He said," some things in life cannot be undone. But, is effect can be reduced to minimal." Similarly, now the lemonade can be used by four persons to meet their thirst.

The reason and solution of each and every problems of life starts with negativity but, always ends with positivity. It's the spirit which makes our mind think in a confident manner.

So be positive and think big...

CHAPTER THIRTEEN

SERVE HUMANITY

A man walking through the park saw a small piece of note hung on the electric pole. The man was curious to know what is written on it and went near it to read it. There he found a note that "I am a poor woman and lost my fifty-rupees note around here on the road. If any one of you happens to finds it kindly bring me to this address. Due to poor eyesight, I can't even see. So, please help."

The man followed the address and saw a very dilapidated hut at that place having a very old lady sitting outside and working. When the lady heard his footsteps she stood up and glanced at him and said in a soft pitch" do you have any work with me dear"? The man replied, "I got your fifty rupees note near the electric pole and am here to return it back". The lady was very amazed and conveyed him that there were twenty more people came to her to return her fifty rupees note. She said that she hasn't lost any note of fifty rupees. She also claimed that the note was not put on by her as she doesn't even know how to read and write.

After listening this man was yet to leave and go, the lady shouted" kindly tear that piece of note on the way back". The man thought that may be some kind hearted person has put it to help the lady. Twenty more persons went to the lady but nobody has torn the note. The man went to his way without tearing the note in a hope of some more help to the old poor lady.

The very topic teaches a lot about humanity and love. Serving others is a boon for our life which very les person get. Help and serve humanity............

CHAPTER FOURTEEN

FIND BEAUTY EVERYWHERE

I remember ones my english teacher said that “there are two words one is ’pretty‘ and another word is ’beautiful‘, she termed that though the very two words sounds simiar but carries a very deep meaning in them. Here, pretty refers to the outsider beauty of a person or his physical appearance but, the term beauty is the pure sole and qualities in a person or anything in the universe. The very day I got to know about the conceptual difference between pretty and beautiful.

My main motive on writing in this topic is that you can find beauty everywhere but the beauty needs to be searched.The earth itself is a concept of beauty. not only for its appearance but for its qualities in nature. But, I never say that eath isn’t pretty. Yes, it is and it will be. But the beauty is that part which matters the most.

we live in a place where people carry negetivity, tension, anxity leading to different chronic and other health problems. But to neutralise we need to be positively charged. And it is none other than the positive vibes. A person having a positive thinking is the only person happy in this universe. The laugh is the only stress releaser of an person in tension.

In other words, I mean to say that we must be able to find beauty in each and every place. And which is earlier defined as positivity. life has no bound. Nobody can predict life cycle but can take a little step to erect it.

Atlast. I would conclude by this piece by saying that "be positive and make others also to be positive. which in the sence will make beauty available everywhere".........

CHAPTER FIFTEEN

GET GOOD AT ASKING

Last week going through an article about a person who is very eager to know about different things. And the most interesting thing about him is that he is illiterate. This made me realize that though he is an illiterate person but then too he is not ashamed of anything to anyone.

The very day I noticed one of my friends that he is not at all good at studies and even not fond of discussion of studies with friends and batch mates. I asked him, `` why don't you participate in the study discussion"? I thought it would be helpful for him for improving his focus in studies.

He answered me that ``I am an introvert and do not like to discuss about anything privately among a group of peoples". He was afraid that they would make joke of him. I told him that nobody can make his ability down by passing jokes. And he also agreed upon it.

The very next day I saw him interacting about studies in the discussion session. My happiness was of no bound because he was my best friend. And his success was rose bed for me. That day he told me that the interaction was very nice and interesting. All others were very interactive. From that day onwards till now he is the best speaker among them.

After the final result of class 10th came, I was surprised to see that his name was in that second rank in the best ten list securing a mark percent of 96. The very day I got to know that asking about something to someone doesn't makes you dumb. Rather, the personality of eagerness to learn arises from you.

At last, I would conclude by saying all the beloved readers to be frank and free in asking things to others. Which would lead you to positivity, rather than negativity...................

Author's Request

Mr. AMRIT WOULD LOVE TO HEAR FROM ALL THE READERS ABOUT THE IMPACT THIS BOOK PUT ON YOU IN TRANSFORMING YOUR LIFE.

HE WOULD ALSO BE VERY EAGER TO KNOW ABOUT SOME CHANGES OR MODIFICATIONS TO BE NEEDED.

KINDLY PUT YOUR REVIEWS AT:

amritnanda2002@gmail.com.

With regards from the author:

Amrit Nanda

9 798885 464482